THE PRO KNOW-HOW™ BOOK OF

21st Century
Book
Cover
Design

A. Michael Shumate

21st Century Book Cover Design

21st Century Book Cover Design
by A. Michael Shumate
Elfstone Press
Cardigan, Prince Edward Island, Canada

ISBN 9780973933383

Book cover designs are rarely credited as to the specific designer. Even so, any designer whose work is shown herein may request credit shown for said work by contacting (ElfstonePress@gmail.com) and credit will be shown in the next edition of this book.

Feedback is also actively sought on other corrections or new examples of principles spoken of in this book.

Pro Know-How™ Books are not written for dummies or for complete idiots. Instead, they are written by experienced professionals for people who have aspirations to acquire skills at a professional level through study and applied effort.

Note on Resolution of Images
Normally in a print book the resolution is made fine so that there are no visible pixels. However, since the whole point of this book is to show that on-screen images of books have very few pixels to show content, the resolutions used for those images are deliberately held to the original screen resolutions.

Contents

CHAPTER 1:
Evolution of Book Covers

The first books were made of clay tablets, strips of bamboo and later, on scrolls of parchment, with obvious drawbacks. These books mostly had no covers.

At the beginning of the Christian Era people began to use the codex style of book, multiple sheets bound along one side. There was a need to identify and protect the book's contents. This would be written on an extra sheet at the front of the book with a protector sheet often added to the back. Parchment like the book's pages was too weak for good protection and so heavier leather, wood and even metal covers were used to not only protect, but to adorn these books.

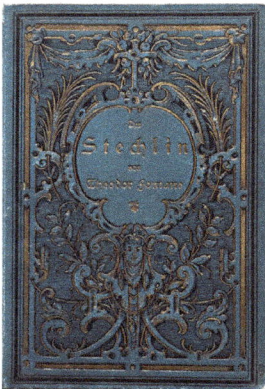

With the advent of printing and the proliferation of books, covers were still needed to identify and protect books with typical coverings being leather or cloth over heavy solid cardboard.

Then as the book industry expanded in the 20th century, the marketing potential of covers began to be exploited more.

Since cloth was harder to print on, a paper jacket was printed and wrapped around the hardcover book and continues to be done today. Libraries, wishing to protect these paper covers, often wrap those paper jackets

with clear plastic. Paperback book covers are well used for their natural marketing potential.

Aside from illustration and design styles, not much has changed in the realm of book cover design for the last half of the 20th century. Even with the popularization of ebook readers in the beginning of the 21st century, none of that required a significant change in book cover design. But there is a needed change now, not because of the way books are made or read but because of the way they are sold.

1.1 21st Century Cover Design

As of 2015, Amazon.com alone sells 41% of all new book unit sales and 65% of all books sold, new or backlist, hardcover, paperback or ebook. Add to that Amazon's various online competitors and we can safely say that at least three quarters of all books are bought online. Barnes and Noble, the largest physical bookstore chain announced

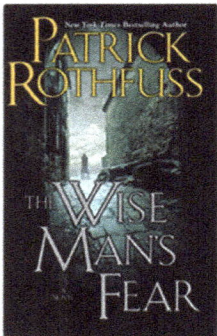

Size of covers on Amazon on each book's "Home Page" 267 pixels high (2¹/₁₆")

Result when searching for a specific book and featured similar books on a home page: 160 pixels high (1¼")

Paid featured ads of related titles on a home page 100 pixels high (¾")

Customers Who Bought This Item Also Bought

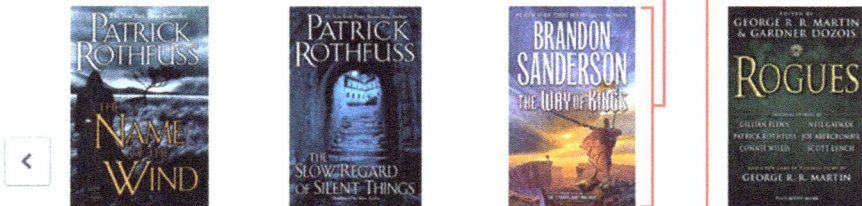

Sponsored Products Related To This Item (What's this?)

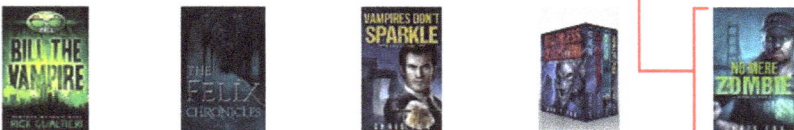

in 2013 that it will close twenty stores a year for the next ten years (source: Harvard Political Review).

Let me be clear, I'm not saying that ebooks are taking over the book readers market. I'm saying that ebook or physical, most books now are *bought* online.

How does that require a change in book cover design?

If you search for a specific book title at Amazon, its cover will be shown at 160 pixels high on a page that also shows similar titles. That is only just over on inch high on a typical computer screen and only three-quarters of an inch high or smaller on a typical handheld device.

iPhone 5S screen resolution is 284 pixels/inch

In Amazon email promos, covers are as small as 140 pixels high

that's only 0.493"

it's less than 1/2"

People who have accounts with Amazon and have bought books may receive email promos based on what books they have either bought or searched for in the past. The covers on those promos may be smaller than one half inch high.

Any way you cut it, there are many legitimate cover designs that may work well on a nine inch cover but just won't work on a one inch cover.

That's the crux of the whole issue. Even if people buy the hardcover, most of them are going to *buy it* based, in part, on a 1 inch rendering of that cover. And if the cover doesn't grab the buyer at 1 inch, the buyer may get a different book, based on its 1 inch cover instead.

Here is the key: If a cover doesn't work at 1 inch tall, it doesn't work at all.

Why? Because that's how the majority of sales are made today. It was never that way in the past but that's the way it is now. And it isn't likely to change. Pining for the good old days when customers viewed full sized covers will not change the reality of marketing books in the 21st century.

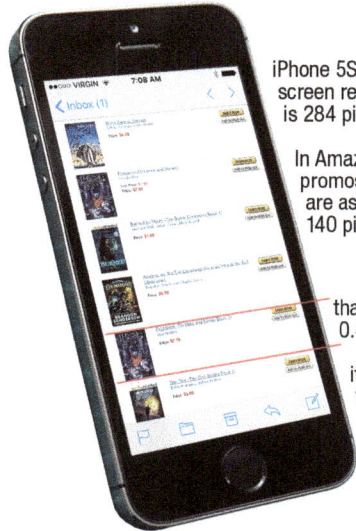

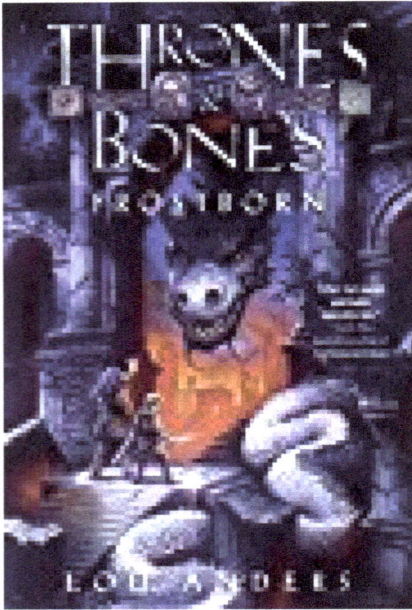

At left is a cover that works reasonably well at 160 pixels high, shown enlarged pixel for pixel. But as first viewed by a typical online shopper, this will only be one inch tall or shorter. Remember that the small number of pixels is important but the small size at which a cover is most likely viewed is an even more important reason to change how we design book covers.

Pixel-for-pixel this is a typical 160 pixel high cover. Some things survive, some don't.

1.2 The Secret to Bestseller Status

Even though cover design is the subject of this book, covers are *not* the number one factor in making a book into a bestseller.

Word-of-mouth is.

And what generates that word of mouth? A great book, its content. People find a book they love and tell their friends, "You *have* to read this." That's the power of word-of-mouth. No book has ever become a bestseller without word-of-mouth.

But what gets those first readers to read a book to start off that cascading word-of-mouth phenomena?

Ah! That's where the cover plays its part. Covers have to convince people who have never heard of a particular book that it is something they will like.

Whoever said, "You can't judge a book by its cover," never tried to sell books. And selling a book is precisely what book covers are all about.

1.3 A Cover's Job

There are four possible tasks a book cover can fulfill. Let's list them in order of importance:

1. Convey the book's title

2. Convey the author's name

3. Convey something about the book's genre, mood, plot or subject

4. Be different, stand out from the crowd

Those tasks have always been the test of a cover's marketability, whether publishers—or their designers—understood it or not. Assuming the quality or content of two different books was comparable, covers that succeeded at more of those four tasks have always sold more books. It never was about winning design awards.

It should be obvious that creating a cover that can do all of those things on a 1 inch cover will require skill, focus and discipline, even tough people do it all the time now. If you can't manage all four, aim for the first three, or at least the first two. But at the bare minimum, if a book cover can't manage the number one task, to convey the book title, it is not going to sell many books.

Some designers get fixated on novelty, thinking this should be the number one quality, but they are mistaken, as the sales of those books will show.

Some people think that the order of those tasks is interchangeable. True, a few big name authors may have their names more prominent than the title, but aside from that, the order of priorities above will always be the best. Being different will never trump conveying the book's title or author's name.

1.4 Back to Basics

Most of the issues of good cover design come down to some visual common sense. As in all areas of human endeavor, common sense in design is surprisingly uncommon.

We live in a graphic savvy culture. Design infuses everything from the gadgets we use to communicate and play, to the clothes we wear, to the bottle our shampoo comes in. Every brochure we pick up, every ad in a magazine, every commercial on TV is designed. It is said that the average person now is exposed to more than 3,000 images a day.

But just because we eat every day doesn't mean we know how to cook.

We'll begin this book with a few fundamental principles of graphic design. Some who consider themselves experienced designers may be tempted to skip this section but I would encourage them not to do so.

Just because we **EAT** every day doesn't mean we know how to **COOK**

If they have learned true principles, through their own trial and error, they may know those principles on a more intuitive level than on a rational level. Making those principles more concrete can only solidify what they already know and may also give them the language and framework to explain those principles to others such as coworkers, illustrators, photographers or clients. That can only be a plus.

To those who think they are so full of creativity that they need not learn such principles at all, I challenge them to refute the logic of these principles *after* examining them. They may find new insights that could change their careers for the better. Why would anyone not want to be a more effective designer?

And if I am wrong, challenge me and convert me to your way of thinking.

CHAPTER 2:

Fundamental Design Principles

2.1 Nature of Creativity

There has been a tendency in recent decades to equate creativity with something new and different. But focusing on the new and different may distract us from the essential part of creativity: the solving of a problem. Creativity, in and of itself, has become a pursuit of some misguided folk, especially in the realm of design.

I have seen some immature designers proudly display their "solution" confident that it will be seen as being creative, in spite of the fact that it fails to solve the problem at hand. They sometimes have consciously avoided a workable solution just because "it's been done."

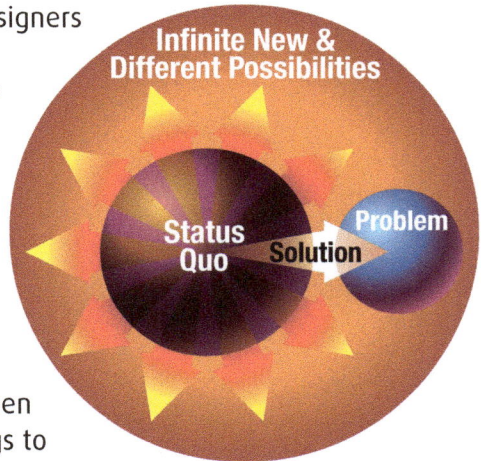

Infinite New & Different Possibilities

Status Quo — Solution → Problem

How sad.

If I have a jar that I can't get open I might try any number of things to unscrew the lid. I might pry a stout knife blade or can opener tip around the rim to loosen it. I might wrap rubber bands around the lid to increase my grip as I try to twist it off. I might run warm water over the metal lid, but not the glass, to get the metal to expand and loosen.

None of those are new and different and, therefore, might be rejected by someone obsessed with "being creative." Instead such a misguided soul might take the jar and smash it on the floor. That's new and different! Yes, but if the jar had any kind of food inside, it would now be inedible. In any case, there will be a mess to clean up.

New and different? Granted. A creative solution? No.

Why? The problem didn't get solved. In fact, a new problem is created.

Don't get me wrong, novelty is good. But it does not trump all other considerations.

2.2 The Purpose of Graphic Design

Ask a dozen people what is the purpose of graphic design and you may get a dozen answers. Many of them will say things like "Make things look fancy," or "Make things look cool," or even "Make it look beautiful." Those are often what happens in good graphic design, but the bottom line is this: Graphic design's job is to help Communicate. It does that job by attracting attention to the message and organizing that message. It uses tools like imagery and type to get across that message and designers must always be mindful of the media or output (in this case, the aforementioned one inch high—or less—book cover seen through a screen of pixels).

Those four contributors are the means to communication, not the end itself; communication is always the end.

Anything that gets in the way of communication is not good graphic design, even if it's fancy, cool or beautiful. In fact, Fancy, Cool or Beautiful can, at times, get in the way of communication.

Instead of those qualities, good graphic design will most often be achieved by following this maxim: Less is More. Put another way, Simplicity is the Soul of Good Design.

Once you learn the truth of this saying, you may stop asking yourself, "What do I need to add to this design?" Instead, you will ask, "What can I omit from this design?" That is what you must do to design effective 1 inch covers.

2.3 Beware BYC Design

There are so many glittering buttons, figuratively speaking, in our modern software: tools, filters or effects. They all beg to be used. But using a particular effect should only be done if it improves the design. Almost the worst reason for employing a filter or some other effect is "Because you Can."

2.4 Beware JTDB Design

Only slightly better is JTBD Design, "Just to Be Different."

Not that novelty is a bad thing. It's great if it doesn't cause other problems like bad legibility, poor reproduction, or greater costs for the client. Not acting in the client's best interest is inherently unprofessional. Measured against the possible downsides, novelty alone can be a poor bargain.

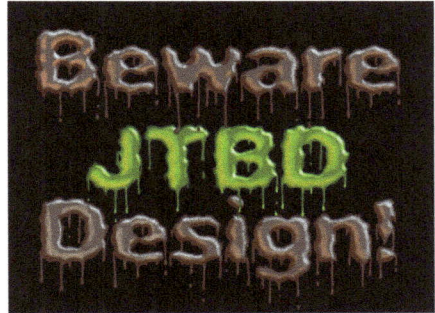

Beware of "Just to Be Different" Design. (Given the moral of this story, this kitschy type treatment is ironically appropriate.)

2.5 Color and Contrast

Being able to *easily* read something is legibility, whether it be words or images. Legibility is a function of contrast.

And contrast is a function of value.

Hue and saturation, while beautiful and visually unique, do not give meaningful contrast to type or images. Only value does.

Surprint 10%	20%	30%	40%	50%
10%	20%	30%	40%	50%
	90%	80%	70%	60%
100% Reverse	90%	80%	70%	60%

A good tool for accurately describing a value is a tint percentage, developed in the printing industry. Halftone tints cover an area with small uniform grid of dots on a paper, often smaller than can be seen with the naked eye. In a 70% halftone tint, for instance, 70% of the paper area is covered in ink and only 30% of the paper has no ink. These halftone tint percentages should be second nature to graphic designers.

100% over 80% = 20% difference:	Insufficient
45% over 80% = 35% difference:	Marginal
30% over 80% = 50% difference:	Adequate
20% over 80% = 60% difference:	Excellent
100% over 60% = 40% difference:	Marginal
40% over 60% = 20% difference:	Insufficient
25% over 60% = 35% difference:	Marginal
0% over 60% = 60% difference:	Excellent
100% over 30% = 70% difference:	Excellent
65% over 30% = 35% difference:	Marginal
50% over 30% = 20% difference:	Insufficient
10% over 30% = 20% difference:	Insufficient

Here we have examples of contrast from excellent to marginal to insufficient. Smaller size magnifies the deficiencies of marginal or insufficient contrast. Also note that the excellent contrast type shown here is only the lowest excellent contrast differential of 60%. Contrast of 70%, 80%, 90% or 100% would, of course, be even easier to read. 60% must be considered the outside limit for excellent contrast. Why would anyone settle for less?

Black on white is as much contrast as we can have, both on a printed page or on a digital screen. It is a 100% difference.

Anything above a 60% contrast differential is excellent contrast. 40% contrast differential is minimal. Anything below that is just not going to give good legibility.

These thresholds are even more important when size or distance make the type small. Then one can plainly see the need for excellent contrast differential.

Can a person eventually figure something out at a low contrast?

Yes, but it isn't easy. And if the purpose of graphic design is to aid communication, why would anyone deliberately use less than excellent contrast (60% difference or more) for anything important in a design?

It is mathematically impossible to have any type achieve a 60% contrast differential over a 50% background. Can't happen. So mid value backgrounds are going to give problems. Instead, any background that will have type over it should either be dark or light in order to have the opposite value type over it.

Remember that size also makes a difference in these legibility calculations. The smaller something is, the greater the need for excellent contrast.

0%	10%	20%	30%	40%	50%	60%	70%	80%	90%	100%
White	White	White	White	White	White	White	White	White	White	White
10%	10%	10%	10%	10%	10%	10%	10%	10%	10%	10%
20%	20%	20%	20%	20%	20%	20%	20%	20%	20%	20%
30%	30%	30%	30%	30%	30%	30%	30%	30%	30%	30%
40%	40%	40%	40%	40%	40%	40%	40%	40%	40%	40%
50%	50%	50%	50%	50%	50%	50%	50%	50%	50%	50%
60%	60%	60%	60%	60%	60%	60%	60%	60%	60%	60%
70%	70%	70%	70%	70%	70%	70%	70%	70%	70%	70%
80%	80%	80%	80%	80%	80%	80%	80%	80%	80%	80%
90%	90%	90%	90%	90%	90%	90%	90%	90%	90%	
Black	Black	Black	Black	Black	Black	Black	Black	Black		

As it turns out in practical terms, the cutoff for surprinting versus reversing type is not at the 50% divide (red line). It's closer to the 35% mark (cyan line). That just happens to be at the Golden Section. Although a person can read black type over a background darker than 35%, it becomes oppressive. So there is inherently about twice the range of values over which reversing is preferable to surprinting.

Black reflects no light, an abscence of stimulus
Black reflects no light, an abscence of stimulus
Black reflects no light, an abscence of stimulus
White relects light, and is a very strong stimulus
White relects light, and is a very strong stimulus
White relects light, and is a very strong stimulus

It just works out that way. But why?

White is pure light or the reflection of light such as off white paper. Black, on the other hand, is the absence of light or the absorption of light on paper. So white is a stimulus to our eyes and black is an absence of stimulus. It should be self evident that a stimulus is more

Every color has a hue, a degree of saturation and a value all bundled together. And so value is part of every color. Designers can save themselves years of fruitless trial and error by just thinking of colors as values when choosing them in a design to assure sufficient contrast. As with other principles in this section, size has a direct bearing on how disastrous mediocre contrast may be to a design. Type with marginal contrast at larger sizes becomes quite illegible when the type is smaller.

noticeable than a non-stimulus. This is why there is a greater range of reverse combinations than surprint combinations.

2.6 The Dreaded V Words

If you have type over backgrounds and the two colors are close in both hue and value, the type will appear to vanish.

If you have type over a background and they are very different in hue, but similar in value, the results will vibrate.

Both are negative outcomes for communication and should be avoided in all situations. The key is that there is a similarity of value, very far from the 60% minimum contrast differential for excellent contrast.

2.7 Busy Backgrounds

A busy background would be one with both light and dark elements in it. Busy backgrounds are the worst thing there is for legibility. The bottom line is this: nothing works over a busy background.

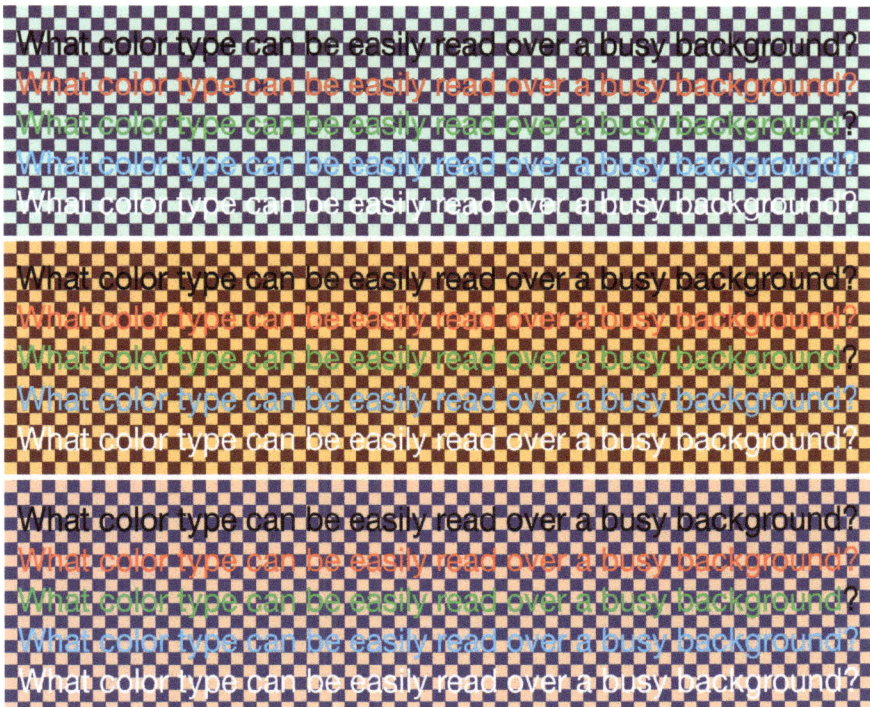

What color type can be easily read over a busy background?
What color type can be easily read over a busy background?
What color type can be easily read over a busy background?
What color type can be easily read over a busy background?
What color type can be easily read over a busy background?

What color type can be easily read over a busy background?
What color type can be easily read over a busy background?
What color type can be easily read over a busy background?
What color type can be easily read over a busy background?
What color type can be easily read over a busy background?

What color type can be easily read over a busy background?
What color type can be easily read over a busy background?
What color type can be easily read over a busy background?
What color type can be easily read over a busy background?
What color type can be easily read over a busy background?

There is a line of text above that reads, "What color type can be easily read over a busy background?" The answer is there is no color that will work, so just don't put type over a busy background. Ever!

This does not mean that all type needs to be over plain backgrounds, they just can't be on backgrounds with large swings in value.

However, if all parts of a background, are either all dark or all light, a good contrast for type can be achieved

However, if all parts of a background, are either all dark or all light, a good contrast for type can be achieved

2.8 Widely Varying Backgrounds

Gradients used to be difficult to achieve but not any more. Designers afflicted with BYC design (because you can) will run into problems if they don't pay attention to the values inherent in every stage of a gradient. If a gradient includes both light and dark areas, then there is no color of text that will avoid at least a part of it being difficult or impossible to read. Gradients can be used if they stay all in the dark range or all in the light range with any type over them in the opposite value.

What color is easily read over widely varying backgrounds?
What color is easily read over widely varying backgrounds?
What color is easily read over widely varying backgrounds?
What color is easily read over widely varying backgrounds?
What color is easily read over widely varying backgrounds?

What color is easily read over widely varying backgrounds?
What color is easily read over widely varying backgrounds?
What color is easily read over widely varying backgrounds?
What color is easily read over widely varying backgrounds?
What color is easily read over widely varying backgrounds?

What color is easily read over widely varying backgrounds?
What color is easily read over widely varying backgrounds?
What color is easily read over widely varying backgrounds?
What color is easily read over widely varying backgrounds?
What color is easily read over widely varying backgrounds?

Some portion of each line of type above is difficult or impossible to read. This is because the values of the type and the backgrounds in that spot are too close. Real legibility is a function of contrast and contrast is a function of value.

2.9 The Doctrine of Coincide or Contrast

This principle has a multitude of applications for a range of choices a designer must make such as fonts, layout and image style.

For instance, it will always be easier to use one font with size and weight to

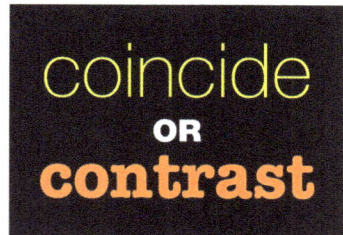

coincide
OR
contrast

differentiate than to use two different fonts. When using fonts, if they are not going to coincide, they should contrast each other.

For this reason, using two different serif fonts together should be avoided. They will not coincide but will be too similar to contrast. Likewise using two different sans serif fonts together should be avoided for the same reason.

Getting two different serif fonts to work together is very difficult. They don't coincide and they are too close to contrast.

Getting two different sans serif fonts to work together is very difficult. They don't coincide and they are too close to contrast.

Georgia and Berhard Modern Std (same point size).

Helvetica Neue LT Light and Gill Sans (same point size).

When selecting different fonts to use together, they should either coincide or contrast.

Serif Headlines Work With Sans-serif Text

Bold Subheads Can Be the Same Size as Text

Text can be in Roman or Light weight and the same size as subheads. The principle is to have as few type differentiators as your material will support. Remember SIMPLICITY is the soul of good design. Reserve the use of italics for *emphasis* within a block of text.

Sans-serif Headlines Work With Serif Text

Bold Subheads Can Be the Same Size as Text

Text can be in Roman or Light weight and the same size as subheads. The principle is to have as few type differentiators as your material will support. Remember SIMPLICITY is the soul of good design. Reserve the use of italics for *emphasis* within a block of text.

Because they so different, a serif can usually contrast nicely with a sans serif font and vice versa.

While using **bold** or *italic* in the same font are fine for emphasis, using alternate width variants poses the same problem: Not enough contrast but too different to coincide.

Bold and italic variants were made to be used with the font they belong to. But not so with Extended or Condensed variants; as different designs they will neither coincide nor contrast enough with the base font.

In a layout items should also either coincide or contrast. Being just a little misaligned draws attention to itself and looks more like an oversight than a deliberate design decision. As such, it takes away from the goal of communication and should be avoided. The messenger is not more important than the message.

Graphic Design

4.2" 3.8"

Graphic design is the methodology of visual communication, and problem-solving through the use of type, space and image. The field is considered a subset of visual communication and communication design, but sometimes the term "graphic design" is used interchangeably with these due to overlapping skills involved. Graphic designers use various methods to create and combine words, symbols, and images to create a visual representation of ideas and messages. A graphic designer may use a combination of typography, visual arts and page layout techniques to produce a final result. Graphic design often refers to both the process (designing) by which the communication is created and the products (designs) which are generated.

Common uses of graphic design include identity (logos and branding), publications (magazines, newspapers and books), print advertisements, posters, billboards, website graphics and elements, signs and product packaging. For example, a product package might include a logo or other artwork, organized text and pure design elements such as images, shapes and color which unify the piece. Composition is one of the most important features of graphic design, especially when using pre-existing materials or diverse elements.
--*Wikipedia*

CHAPTER 3:
Fundamental Illustration Principles

3.1 Illustration Concepts

It may surprise you to learn it, but of all of the millions of different illustrations you may have seen in your life, there are only four different kinds of concepts. I'm not talking about either style or technique here but the concept, the idea being visually portrayed.

These concepts apply to illustration that is painted as well as to photography.

3.2 Narrative Concepts

This concept shows an event, a situation or a scene that actually happens in the story or subject being illustrated. Narrative is the oldest and most common form of illustration. We see it—sometimes with editorially exaggerated sizes—on the walls of Egyptian tombs and other art: King Narmer about to whack an enemy king with his war mace; King Akhenaton playing with his daughter while his wife, Nefertiti looks on.

Narrative is virtually the only concept used for children's picture books.

The key to distinguishing Narrative concepts from other concepts is that the interaction or event shown really occurs in the story. Think of it as a single freeze-frame from a movie. It is not editorializing about the story, just showing some important moment in the story. In fact, for a narrative approach to be successful, from a marketing point of view, it should show a moment in the story which is particularly intriguing.

A book cover for Melville's famous novel Moby-Dick could picture a white whale charging a much smaller harpoon boat. Since this actually takes place in the story it is a prime example of Narrative approach.

A poster for the comic opera, "La Gordona Canta" (The Fat Lady Sings), could show the leading character, Porkanella, singing to the poor, squashed Thinetto who she has pinned against the wall. Since this scene actually happens in the plot of the opera, it is a legitimate narrative approach.

In a magazine article about harmonious divorces, a narrative approach illustration might show a couple sitting amicably at a table with a lawyer.

For the "Three Little Pigs," one might show the third little pig building his sturdy house or when the big bad wolf tries huffing and puffing to blow down that house with the three little pigs in it.

For "Rapunzel," it might be the moment when the prince climbs up to her tower window using her hair.

The key is that these things all actually happen in their respective stories.

One caveat: don't give away story endings. Spoilers on book covers ruin it for readers and hurt sales. You wouldn't show the big bad wolf running away, holding his burnt bum. Nor would you show Captain Ahab's body wrapped in harpoon ropes around the white whale.

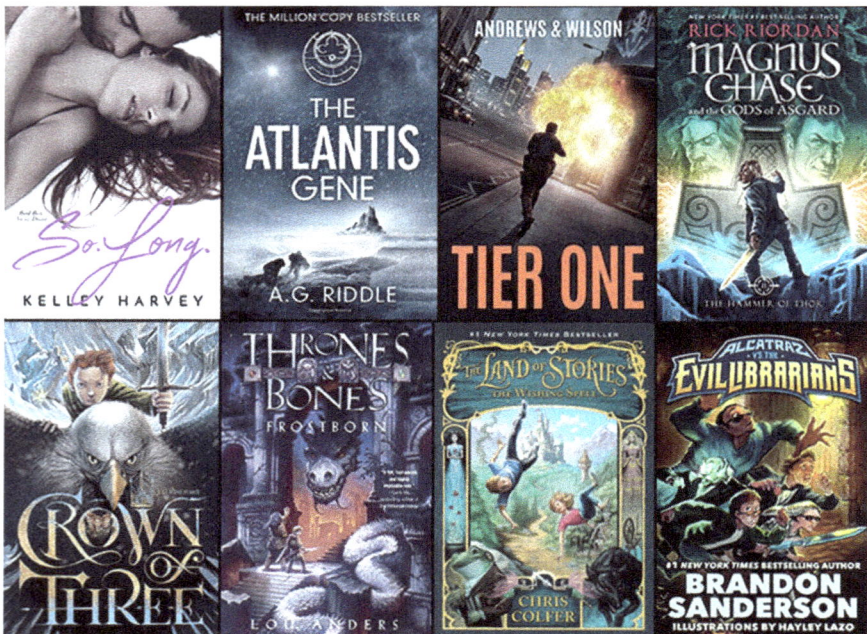

Each of these covers uses a narrative concept illustration. Note that in this sense, illustration can mean either a painted (any kind of hand made image) or photography. Above we have a romance novel, two thrillers and five in middle grade or young adult genres. Each one shows a situation that actually happens in the story.

3.3 Cast or Character Concepts

This concept doesn't show any action from a story but merely shows the main character or cast of characters in the story. This approach is restricted to only show the persons and/or objects and/or places discussed in a story or subject without reference to events in the story. The key to the Cast or Character approach is that the visual elements do not interact in the picture plane.

For the cover of Dickens' *Oliver Twist* you might show a poor street boy looking distressed.

For *Pride and Prejudice* you might show Elizabeth Bennet and Mr. Darcy, but not talking or interacting at all.

The cover of the novel *The Brothers Karamazov* could show the four brothers' faces side by side and even add the family mansion in the background; but showing no action and no situation from the story.

A magazine article about "Burned-out Housewife Syndrome" could show a woman with a worn-down and inexpressive look.

The cover of a book on archaeology could feature the face mask of Pharaoh Tutankhamen.

A book about responses to terrorism, entitled *A Test of Wills*, might feature with the portraits of Osama Bin Laden, George Bush, Tony Blair and Saddam Hussein. The men's faces are merely shown with no interaction.

To the novice, Cast/Character approaches sometimes don't even seem worthy of the term concept. After all, it is just showing the Character or Cast of Characters from a story. But in the hands of a skillful art director, illustrator and/or photographer, a Cast/Character illustration may be the most effective for a particular use.

Most of the covers for *Cyrano de Bergerac* have only shown Cyrano with his huge nose and little else. Album covers for the opera "Boris Goudinov" most often show a portrait of the troubled Czar Boris without any other reference to the story.

In the end, an illustration is more than concept. It is a marriage of style, media and concept.

Movie posters are often done in a montage approach, which is just a variation of the Cast/Character conceptual approach. One of the more famous posters for Star Wars (there were several different posters used in different cities) shows Luke and Leia, R2D2 and C3PO, Darth Vader and the death star. None of the characters are interacting with each other. Many characters are shown in different visual scales so that it is obvious that they are not being shown in the same three-dimensional space; instead, they are in "montage space."

As we will discuss later, montages do not survive well on a 1 inch cover and are no longer as effective as they once were when book covers were typically first seen at full size, in the potential customer's hand. But for other uses, such as movie posters, montages are still viable.

Cast/Character concepts give minimal or no plot and can show people and sometimes a location. The Cast/Character approach is the most popular concept for romance novels and are frequently used on covers for historical novels and virtually every other genre of novel and many non-fiction books.

3.4 Allegorical Concepts

This concept may use invented characters to show an underlying principle or moral of the story. Conversely, real characters from the story may be shown in an unreal situation. Sometimes even emotions or inanimate objects may be personified. The key for this kind of concept is that these situations don't really happen in the story, but represent the ideas, feelings or morals of the story.

An allegorical concept for a magazine article on US-Canada trade relations could have Uncle Sam (representing the USA) chopping with an axe the crutch that a beaver (representing Canada) is leaning on. These characters are allegorical.

An article on the misuse of power in government agencies (FBI, CIA, Department of Homeland Security, etc.) could show an average looking couple and their children shrinking in fear underneath a large man's menacing shadow.

One of the posters for Star Wars showed a large Darth Vader holding a smaller Princess Leia and Luke Skywalker in his gloved hand. Since Vader is the same general size as Leia and Luke, this concept is showing an unreal situation, one that represents the power of Vader compared to the other characters. It is an allegorical approach.

Contrasting with one narrative example used earlier, we might show the big bad wolf grimacing as he falls into a boiling cauldron that has a pig face on it. This doesn't happen literally in the story but represents an idea or allegory of the story.

For Rapunzel we might see her tied from neck to toe in her own hair while the prince is trying to cut her free with scissors. However, as we have said before, children's illustration almost never uses anything but narrative concepts.

An allegorical cover for *Moby-Dick*, might show Captain Ahab, arms folded with a hateful glare, looking at the giant eye of the white whale who is glaring back.

Allegories can easily become parodies; humor might be the wrong mood for a dramatic book and care must be taken to project an accurate mood for the story at hand.

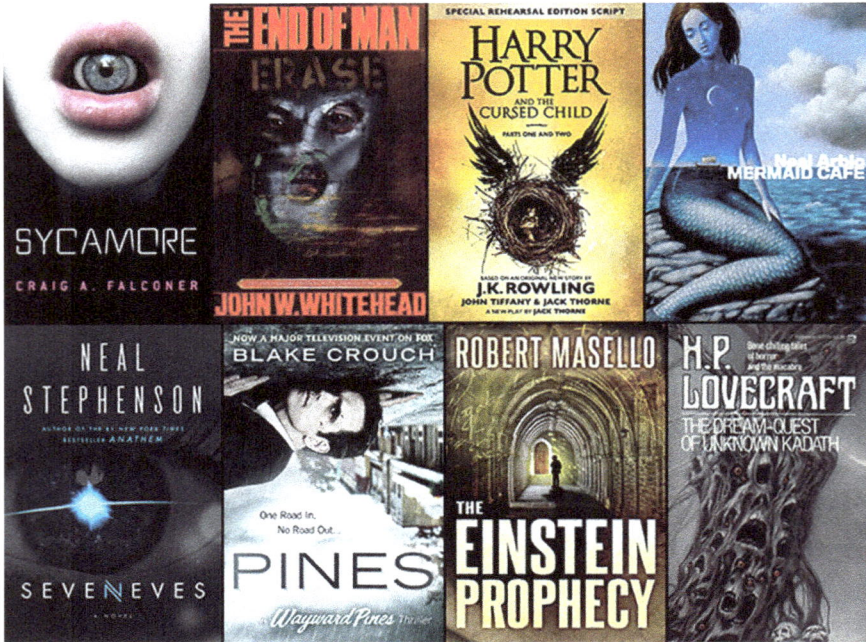

Each of these allegorical concept covers shows an unreal situation that does not happen in their respective books, but rather communicates a concept or mood from the story.

3.5 Symbolic Concepts

These are similar to allegorical concepts, but they reduce the comparison to non-personified or nonhuman symbols. The elements are graphic and simple.

For a book on the erosion of the American society the cover might show an American flag with large portions worn or eaten away.

A symbolic cover for a book on investments might show a coin planted in the ground with a hundred dollar bill sprouting from it.

A book titled "Greatest Movie Love Stories," could show several movie projectors, all shining overlapping heart images on the moon.

The key here is to not use people or personified objects, but limit the elements to inanimate objects and graphic symbols.

Each of these covers uses a non-personified image, animal or inanimate object to show a central theme of the story. In today's book marketing reality they often hold up better to small reproduction than more complex visual treatment and can be quite effective.

3.6 More Fruitful Conceptualizing

Knowing that all illustrations use one of these four concepts can be empowering for generating concepts for any illustration task such as book covers. By deliberately trying to develop one or more concepts for an image using each of the four possible conceptual approaches, one can not only develop more concepts to begin with, but, with practice, better quality concepts as well. Be sure to jot down all such visual brainstorming with at least simple thumbnail sketches and notations as needed.

As important as a good concept is, a concept is only really good if it can be successfully combined with the other constraints of the creative mix for that image.

Let's look at the some of those constraints.

• STYLE Will the concept work well with the style or technique chosen or should a different style or technique be selected to better suit a given concept? A frenetic or highly stylized approach may not have the visual detail to show important elements of a particular concept. A given style may not have the "visual language" to show facial expression or period costume, for instance.

• APPROPRIATE MOOD It is important to be honest in the illustration of a subject. Even though there is a budding romance in the movie Star Wars, it would be dishonest to portray it as a love story when it is clearly a science fiction action story. Some movies have been billed as "feel-good" movies when they are really about marital conflict and infidelity and finish far from a happy ending. This is not only dishonest marketing but foolish as well because the persons who might truly find the content appealing are steered away, thinking it is something else.

• CORE IDEA VS. PERIPHERAL Using Star Wars as an example again, there are a few comical moments in the film, but to bill it as a comedy or illustrate the posters for it in a comedic style would be quite a mistake. Likewise, honesty really is the best policy and central ideas should be focused on rather than peripheral ideas, even if the peripheral ideas are found in the work.

• MARKETABLE GRAB This may sound like a contradiction of the foregoing, but the concept should be as interesting as possible. It has to engage people, to peak curiosity, to captivate them. Whatever concept is chosen, it should have appropriate marketability. The interest level must be equal to, or greater than the "price of admission."

Any illustrator who approaches this evaluation process from a position of wealth of concepts, not poverty, will more likely come through with a fine solution in the end. If an art director or an illustrator only has one or two ideas, being honest in evaluating those few ideas becomes more difficult. How much courage does it take to reject an idea because it isn't quite right if that's the only idea you have?

But even when starting with several concepts, if after the evaluation process, you have no ideas that are really workable, you can return to the conceptualizing phase more sensitized to the needs of the particular problem at hand. It can actually be easier the second time around. After you are all warmed up, a good solid concept may emerge more easily.

3.7 Conventions, Styles & Techniques

It is no secret that different book genres often have long-standing conventions regarding their covers. Using an out-of-date approach to cover design is one of the frequent faults with many indie and self published books. They use cover design elements of the books they have read in the past but fail to perceive that covers in their chosen genre are different now.

Romance novels, for instance, historically have used illustrated covers in a realistic style. Now they mostly use photography with almost none of the top 100 romance books using illustration any more. So do romantic comedies. Readers who like those books have become accustomed to certain cover imagery. To use an unconventional cartoon illustration style cover for a serious romance will be going against the trend. In terms of concepts, Romance and Romantic Comedies, Cast/Character covers predominate, executed more often with photography.

The top 100 books in the Mystery, Triller & Suspense genre have a much broader range of cover concepts. Cast/Character are still well represented, but so are Narrative and occasionally Symbolic or Allegorical. Stylistically, they still are mostly photographic or photo realistic illustration.

In the Science Fiction and Fantasy genre there is a higher incidence of illustration to photography. This is understandable since often the subject matter doesn't exist to be photographed. Still, the illustration style tends to be more photographic realism than stylized.

Fantasy novel covers are mostly illustrated but are still photo-realistic in style.

Interestingly, literary fiction has the least use of narrative concepts, favoring instead Cast or Character, Allegorical and Symbolic concepts. There is a broad range of illustration styles as well, not just photography or realistic illustration.

Nonfiction books do use perhaps the broadest range of illustration styles but photography is very popular here as well.

Chapter Books and Middle Grade fiction covers is one segment where illustration dominates and mostly in non-realistic styles, too. But Young Adult books, by comparison, do not use illustration often but favor photography like most of the adult genres.

Style is the visual system for drawing an image. There is virtually no limit to the number of styles. Even so, we can recognize some broad categories such as photographic realism, retro or cartoon. But there are so many hundreds of styles that are possible that describing even a quarter of them would be a daunting task. As we have seen in the above genres, with the exception of Middle Grade fiction, realism or photography is the most common style. That doesn't mean that other styles are incorrect, but it may put off your intended audience if you use a style that is less favored.

Regardless of the style you wish to use, there is one principle that must be observed: do not mix either styles or techniques on a single cover. The resulting disharmony is a mark of amateur art direction and artists.

CHAPTER 4:

Seven Deadly Sins of Book Cover Design

4.1 One Strike and You're Out!

In the past, when most book sales were achieved right from the shelves of bookstores, a front cover certainly was a factor that contributed to initial sales, but so were the blurb and review quotes on the back cover. Having the book already in hand, one was more likely to look at the back cover material. One might be right in saying that back then a batter had three strikes before being out of the running.

But now, given the reality of 21st century book marketing, that the vast majority of sales are online instead of in traditional brick and mortar bookstores, and given the overwhelming tsunami of selection a modern book buyer must wade through, one can say that a cover is the first and most important factor in contributing to initial book sales. A person has to click to see the material that formerly was on the back cover. And if they don't click, that's the end of it. Too many books to filter through.

These days, it's one strike and you're out.

Book covers have always been a method of consumer triage, of sorting through the flotsam to find what you want. That is more true now than ever. Now you only get one strike and you're out of the running for that customer during that online viewing. And remember, the first cover a potential customer is likely to see is only about an inch high or less.

Some publishers opt for additional online marketing exposure, paying to have their cover shown when not directly sought via a "Sponsored Products Related To This Item" listing. These covers are even smaller, less than 3/4 of an inch high!

You can run but you can't hide from the facts of contemporary book marketing. Covers have to do their job under constraints that book cover designers never had to face in the past.

What follows are failings that might legitimately constitute that "one strike and you're out" in a customer's eyes. It may be a little melodramatic but I call each of these design faults "Deadly Sins of Book Cover Design."

These mistakes always did weaken a book cover, but didn't drag a cover down as much because the book was being viewed at full size and only a few inches away. Subtle things could still work.

But not now. Reducing things in size *magnifies* the detriment of each of these faults to fatal proportions.

That's why they're Deadly Sins.

CHAPTER 5:
Deadly Sin of Cover Design #1 Poor Contrast

5.1 I Can't See You

Undoubtedly the most frequent mistake in book cover design is not understanding the basic principle of legibility: that legibility is a function of contrast and contrast is a function of value (see section 2.5 Color and Contrast).

Here we can see in practice the need for excellent contrast (60% to 100% contrast differential) in at least the title and author type. We also see how often artists and photographers—and the art directors they report to—do not understand that you can not get a 60% difference in value from a 50% background; it is mathematically impossible.

The practice of avoiding middle value backgrounds for type is the single easiest way to prevent contrast issues.

The sad thing is that this all-to-common mistake is not just in the ever growing tide of self-published books. No, this is happening within the big five publishing houses who have fine designers who are spending money on quality imagery and even custom rendered type.

Note: All examples in this section are shown at 160 pixels high, which is how big covers are shown in a search or in the "Customers Who Bought This also Bought" section that show on every page in Amazon's book department. This is the most likely size that the majority of book shoppers will first see any cover.

Many of these issues would never come up with proper art direction and instruction to the illustrator or photographer before the images are created. All areas for type should be designated ahead of time to be either dark or light areas.

Top Row: 1. All of the author's name and most of the title is light type over a light background. **2.** Author and title type is verging on a middle value over backgrounds that range from light to dark, giving none of the type excellent contrast and some of it is quite difficult to read. **3.** Dark red title over dark gray or black gives very poor contrast. **4.** Drop shadows try but fail to fix a problem of mid value type over a light to mid value background. **5.** Two and a half letters of this title have good contrast; the rest is mostly mid value type over dark or mid value backgrounds. **6.** This red type is mid value and has poor contrast over the background that is also mostly mid value. **Middle Row: 1.** The title's blue type is darker than mid over a background that is also mostly dark. **2.** Here beautiful custom rendered title type is lost over a busy and mostly mid value background; the authors' type is 3D with half of each character being light over a light background. **3.** In spite of having a separate cartouche for the type, the mid value green title is over a mid value gray. **4.** The deep blue type may look cool but it isn't easy to read. **5.** Light author type over a light sky is nearly invisible. **6.** The author's type is light but much of the background under it is also mid to light. **Bottom Row:** Here are relatively easy fixes (or at least improvements) for most of the contrast issues in the middle row showing that these issues can be successfully overcome with a little attention to this principle and some knowledge.

CHAPTER 6:

Deadly Sin of Cover Design #2 Busy Backgrounds

6.1 Interference

Again we come to the issue of art direction, the function that designers must fulfill when commissioning or supervising the creation of an image, whether illustration or photography. From the prevalence of busy backgrounds it would appear that too many art directors are abdicating their role to oversee the image's creation, as if they turn the artist or photographer loose, then, after the finished product is submitted, see what they can do with it. Instead, proper art direction should include instructions about which areas of an illustration would need to support type, and therefore be either light or dark and never busy.

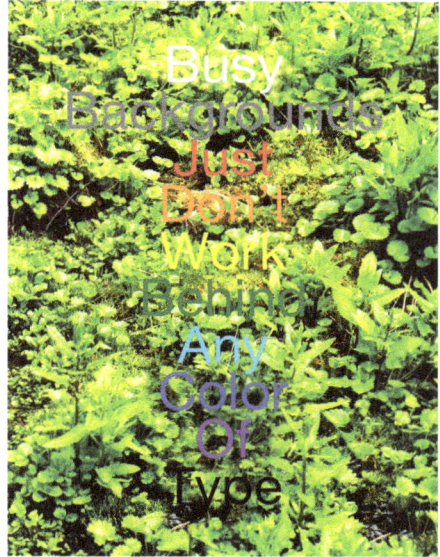

The text above says, "Busy Backgrounds Just Don't Work Behind Any Color Of Type."

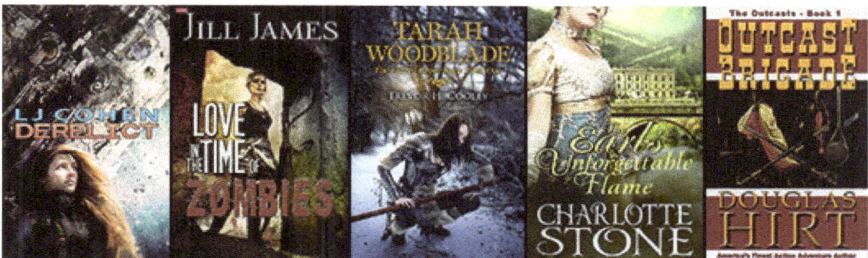

At best, busy backgrounds destroy legibility for only a portion of type, but people reading it for the first time will still have difficulty with it. Light and dark values together under any color of type will compromise its legibility.

It doesn't have to be busy under an entire word for it to be unreadable. Even a busy background under half a word is still disastrous. As with so many of these principles, their effect on legibility is magnified when the words are smaller as seen on covers online.

CHAPTER 7:

Deadly Sin of Cover Design #3: Wimpy Type

7.1 Pixel Mush

Book covers are typically printed at 120 to 150 halftone dots per inch which requires an image of 300 pixels an inch. Most digital handheld devices and computer screens are in the range of 128 pixels per inch. That sounds like a very good resolution for viewing. The real problem is the size at which they are viewed.

Book covers on any digital device, from a desktop computer to a smart phone, are seen through a grid of pixels. When hard edged forms, like type, are viewed through this grid, the edges will be softened because the edge pixels often have to be shared between the type color and the background color. When any shape (like lightweight type) is too thin to be represented by even one whole pixel, the contrast level will also fall. I call this effect "Pixel Mush."

Caxton Light
Times Bold
Helvetica Light
Helvetica Bold

Caxton Light
Times Bold
Helvetica Light
Helvetica Bold

Even though all the original type is black on white, note that when reduced to be rendered with fewer pixels, how much lighter the pixels are with the light weight fonts, thus lowering their contrast. This is the effect of "Pixel Mush." It is why fonts with low mass do not survive reduction as well as fonts with good mass.

How does this principle impact book cover design?

Three design practices will make Pixel Mush more likely when covers are viewed at the standard small online sizes. We'll look at these separately.

7.2 Small Type

It has become very fashionable to understate type. This was a novel thing when covers were typically viewed actual size in one's hands

in the book store. But it is a death knell for modern book covers. Yes, if I have a cover that will be anywhere from seven to twelve inches tall, I can be modest with the type, use lots of white space, be more "designerly" with the cover. But when my canvas shrinks to an inch or less, to make my type smaller than that limited space will allow would be foolish. I would be throwing away legibility. Size matters. And type that is smaller than it needs to be will pay the price online. Every cover must survive and be legible at one inch high. It's just a fact of life in the 21st century.

7.3 No Mass

As was shown in the previous illustration, type with more mass will keep its original contrast better than thin letter forms. That doesn't mean that all type needs to be big, blocky fonts, though that kind of font does very well in size reduction. But it does mean that light weight fonts are worse than Book weight, Book is weaker than Regular, and Regular is not as sturdy as Demi, etc. While it is true that there has been a recent trend away from heavy fonts, that trend carries its own limitations because the need for maximum contrast goes up as mass goes down.

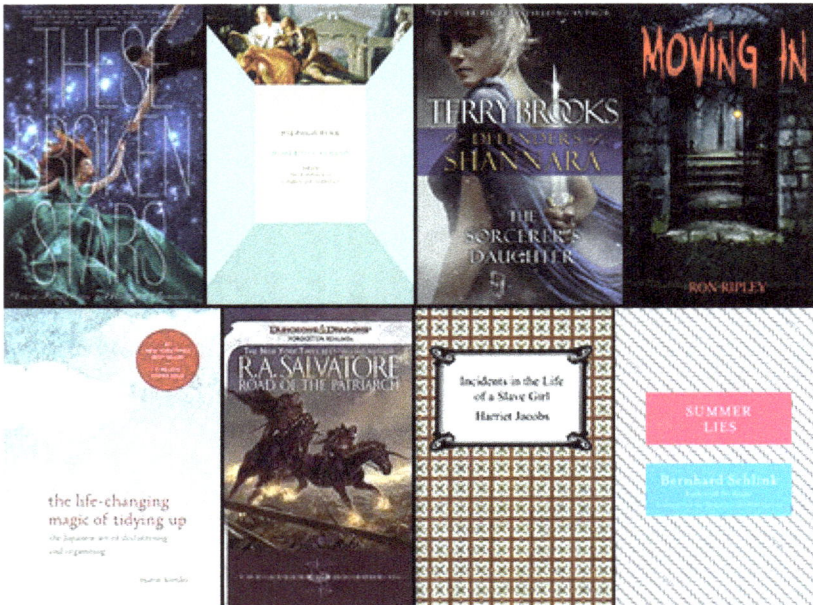

Some of this type is too small and some lacks mass to make them readable with the limited number of pixels through which they will be viewed. Some are further aggravated by other issues such as poor contrast color choices.

7.4 Extra Letterspacing

This is another token of "artsy" type styling, but it causes natural reduction in type size, our first cause of wimpy type. In any word with double letterspacing the type size goes down to approximately 60% of the

Letterspacing
L e t t e r s p a c i n g
L e t t e r s p a c i n g
Letterspacing
L e t t e r s p a c i n g
Letterspacing
Letterspacing
L e t t e r s p a c i n g
Letterspacing

Given a finite horizontal space, type always has to shrink in size to compensate for any extra letterspacing. Couple that with overall size reduction and the type can get so small that there just aren't enough pixels to render it clearly.

original to fit in the same horizontal space.

Each of these author names have been made less legible by using extra letterspacing. Some have been further disadvantaged by being in colors with minimal contrast.

CHAPTER 8:

Deadly Sin of Cover Design #4: Inept Type

8.1 Type Errors That Diminish Contrast

Besides the type issues already discussed, which all center around the lack of sufficient pixels to render type at the original contrast, there are other issues that hinder type's ability to be easily read. These divide into two main categories: 1) type treatment that diminishes contrast, and therefore legibility, and 2) inept type treatment.

8.2 Drop Shadows

Drop Shadows can either reinforce type's legibility or work against it. As mentioned before, in order to get excellent contrast, type needs to be dark over a light background or light over a dark background. Nothing works well over a busy background. To boost contrast, a drop shadow should be closer to the background value than that of the type. Unfortunately, too many designers are apparently so clueless that they sometimes give the drop shadow more contrast than the

Top Row: The drop shadows have greater contrast than the letterforms, not the easiest to read. **Middle Row:** Drop shadow and letters are both in the same value range, making the letters less distinct. **Bottom Row:** The letters have the greatest contrast with the background, and the drop shadow has the least contrast; this will always give the best legibility.

type itself. It is considerably harder to read the drop shadows of words instead of the words themselves. That is what inept designers are doing when the drop shadows have the greatest contrast instead of the letters.

8.3 Glow Effects

The same principles apply to the glow effect: the actual letters need to have the greatest contrast with their background, not the glow.

Top Row: Again we see if the glow has more contrast than the letters, we have to, in effect, read the glow instead of the letters. **Middle Row:** If the glow is in the same value range as the letters, it makes them less distinct. **Bottom Row:** If a glow is used, it should always enhance the contrast of the letters, never detract from them. Reduction in size will always show the error of disregarding this and other good design principles.

8.4 Internal Shading

Now it is extremely easy to embellish type with many effects such as internal shading. As with all other such effects, just being able to do it does not guarantee a better reading experience for the viewer. If shading goes from top to bottom and one half of the letters are in poor contrast, the result will be disastrous, it doesn't matter if it is the tops or the bottoms of the words. Even worse is when each letter is shaded from side to side (which is the default direction for gradients in most graphics software). The only way that inner shading will not destroy or at least compromise legibility is if both colors in the gradient are at the opposite end of the value scale from the background. As with all other issues of contrast, value is the key ingredient.

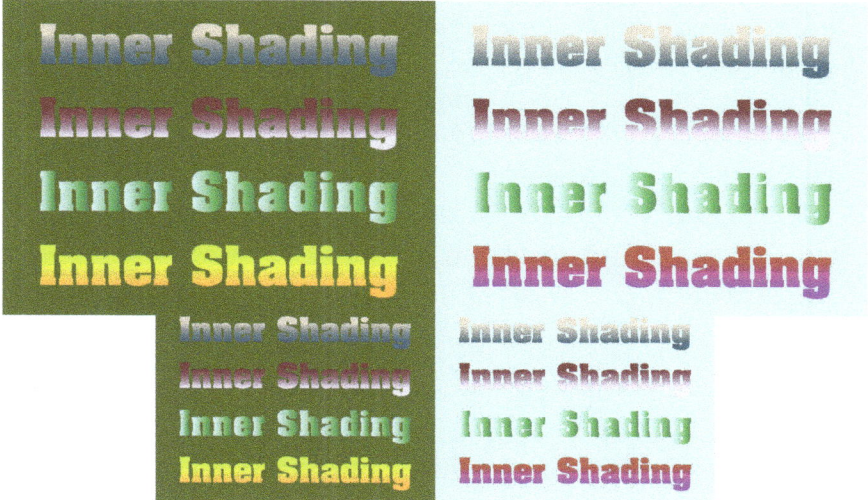

In each of the top three rows on either side part of each letterform is in low contrast with its background because the gradients go between light and dark. If, however, the gradient is limited between mid and light over a dark background, there will be sufficient contrast for all parts of a letterform. Similarly, if the gradient is limited between mid and dark over a light background, the letterforms will have enough contrast as well.

8.5 Amateur Typography

The next group of typographic ineptitudes come from a lack of experience with type itself. These are more of esthetic issues than physical legibility issues. They still have an effect on viewers, although they may not be able to articulate what it is. We are so saturated with good design that when we see amateur treatment it registers with us. Though some of these elements are subtle, they do carry a message, even if it is on a subliminal level.

Before proceeding, it will be helpful to review some basic typographic terms.

Type size is measured from the top of the highest ascender in a font to the lowest descender.

Baseline is the line that most letters appear to rest upon.

X-Height is the height of most lower case letters. Leading is the amount of vertical space between the descenders of one line of type to the ascender of the line of type below it.

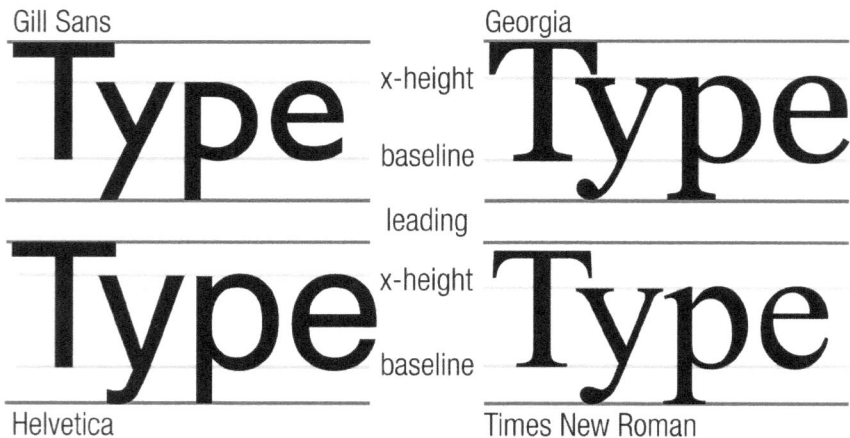

Fonts can appear to be different sizes even though they are the same point size. This comes from the variance in how big the x-height is (from the baseline to the top of most lower case letters) from one font design to another. In these four samples, the x-height of Gill Sans is only 84% that of Helvetica. Note also that the cap height is not always the top edge for a particular font design. In Times, for example, all lower case ascenders like b, d, f, h, etc. (not shown here) are taller than the capitals.

8.6 Fancy Fonts, Scripts, Fad styles

A typical mistake of beginning designers is to opt for fonts that are the latest popular style. It is the nature of fads that they do not remain in vogue for long, and so such fonts can look dated very quickly. Even worse, inexperienced designers may choose fonts that were once popular but now only look passé.

Another common error is using very "fancy" fonts, often trading off legibility for some perceived "cool factor." This is always a bad bargain, because if legibility is sacrificed, the coolness doesn't matter. This is particularly true of script fonts. They are generally much harder to read than either serif or sans serif fonts. Scrip t fonts typically also have much smaller x-heights than most serif or sans serif fonts.

Akzidenz Grotesk	Legibility	Baskerville	Legibility	Arcana	*Legibility*
Dax	Legibility	Bookman	Legibility	Banshee	*Legibility*
Frutiger	Legibility	Ellington	Legibility	Bickham	*Legibility*
Gill Sans	Legibility	Garamond	Legibility	Charme	*Legibility*
Helvetica	Legibility	Georgia	Legibility	Kuenstler	*Legibility*
Myriad Pro	Legibility	Minion Pro	Legibility	Mistral	*Legibility*
Univers	Legibility	Palatino	Legibility	Spring	*Legibility*
Verdana	Legibility	Times New Roman	Legibility	Voluta	*Legibility*

All these font samples are the same point size, including the scripts. Because of the different size of the x-height in the different font designs, some will appear larger than others. Here we can also see the relative lack of legibility inherent in script styles, not only because of the more eccentric shapes of the letterforms, but also because of the tiny x-heights compared to most serif or sans serif fonts.

8.7 Bad Kerning and Leading

Kerning is the adjustment of the horizontal spacing between letters in a word. There is no need of this in normal body text, but when setting type for titles and author names, care must be taken to compensate for different visual effects that happen between certain letter combinations. To fail to do this is the mark of an amateur.

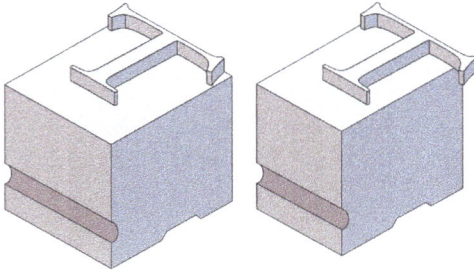

Kerning was so important that from almost the very beginning of metal type printing, special alternate letters were cast in lead so that certain letter pairs could be kerned properly.

Leading is the amount of vertical space between one line of type and the one below it. In body text like this, the usual amount of leading is about 20% of the type size or more. This makes for comfortable reading of large amounts of text and is the default. But that amount of vertical space in a typical large title or author's name will look clumsy.

In most software both the default horizontal spacing for text and the default leading are geared for body text. They look fine there, but when text is enlarged for titles on everything from magazines headlines to poster headlines to book cover titles, those default spaces will look too spread out. That's where kerning and negative leading come in. The goal in these instances is to have the gaps between letters in words look evenly spaced and for these word clusters to hold together visually.

"Tracking" is the term used by most software programs to adjust horizontal letterspacing. A good starting place for titles and author names is to try tracking at -25. Depending on the font design and weight, you may even want to go to a -50.

After that, specific letter pairs (such as Ta, Wo and Le) may need individual tracking to let the second letter come closer to the first. This is accomplished by putting the cursor in the gap between the two letters and using the left arrow and some specialty key (this varies according to the software program). The goal is to get the gaps between letters to look equivalent.

Normal leading for text is way too much for titles and author names. A default leading setting for 30 point type, for instance, might be 36 points. This means there would be 6 points of vertical space between each 30 point line of type. "Solid" leading would be 30 on 30, in other words, no leading added between lines. Negative leading should be used if the type is all caps and whenever descenders of one line do not conflict with the ascenders of the line beneath it. A comfortable amount of space to use between lines is often the width of the strokes in the font. The advantage of taking out this unnecessary space both horizontally and vertically is that the whole type block can be enlarged to fill the same territory, thus increasing its legibility, especially at the reduced size of book covers as seen online.

Natural Letterspacing & Leading	Kerning Applied & Negative Leading	Enlarged to Occupy the Same Vertical Space
Don't Like Tepid Water	Don't Like Tepid Water	Don't Like Tepid Water

1. Large type with default tracking and leading. **2.** Same size type with extra tracking and leading removed (note that descender of the p of Tepid fits nicely between the W and t of Water). **3.** With unnecessary space removed, the type block can be enlarged to use the same vertical space thus increasing legibility significantly.

8.8 Outlining

Putting an outline on type can help with contrast, but it should never take the place of the actual letterforms having good contrast with their background. Reading words by the outlines of the letters instead of the letters themselves is disastrous for legibility. It amounts to visual corruption and in no way is creative, artsy or—pardon the pun—edgy. It's just bad design.

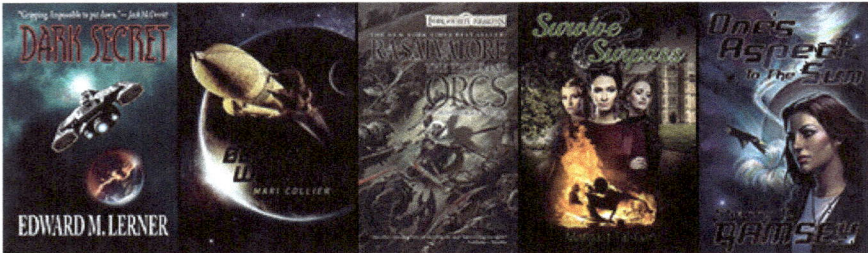

Each of these covers has type that uses an outline to assist with contrast. They fail because it is the letterforms themselves needs the contrast, not just the outlines.

8.9 Too Many Fonts

Given the small amount of text on most book covers, using a single font with only color and/or size to differentiate can result in a very handsome cover. Two different fonts, that contrast nicely (see 2.9 Coincide or Contrast) can also work well.

Beyond that, every additional font carries the risk of making the whole design look like a yard sale. Simplicity is the soul of good design. Calling attention to the design gets in the way of communication.

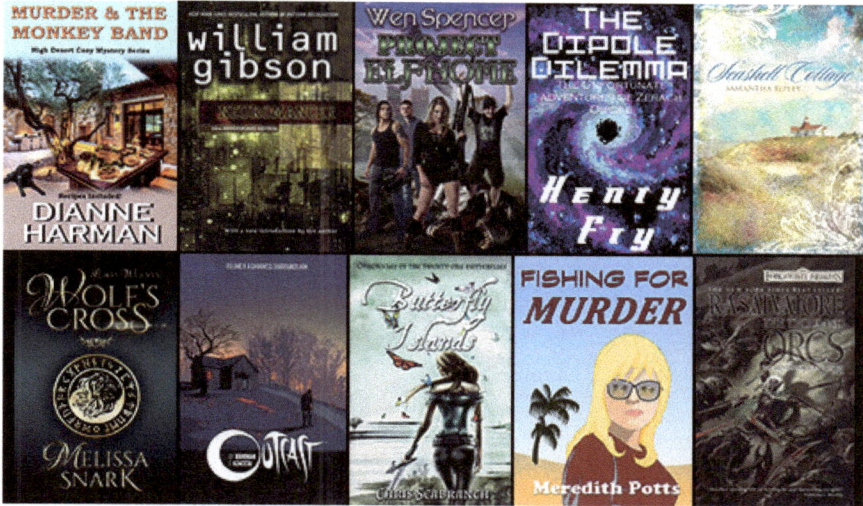

Top Row: 1. Drop shadows can assist with contrast but should never take the place of the letters themselves having good contrast. In this case the letters have minimal contrast and only the drop shadows are left to be read. **2.** The glow around the author type helps with its contrast but the title is entirely unreadable because only the glow has any contrast and not the letters themselves. **3.** Internal shading destroys the legibility of this title. **4.** Ultra modern type often has eccentricities that hinder reading, use with great care. **5.** Script type typically has very small x-height, but there was plenty of space for both the title and author's name to be up to twice a large by stacking the words vertically instead of them being side-by-side. **Bottom Row: 1.** Using a very different capital at the beginning of a word is always disruptive to reading, but it can be pulled off if both fonts are not too difficult to read. **2.** Custom typography is a specialty that not everyone can do well. Here the word should read as Outcast but could be misread as Outraft. The author's name is much too small to read with no good reason; there was plenty of room for larger type. **3.** Aside from the issues of contrast, the first letters in the title words have unnatural gaps between them and their next letters. Kerning should have been applied. **4.** Three different fonts for just the title and author and poorly handled at that. **5.** Here the outlining of the type does not compensate for the type itself having very poor contrast.

There are many ways to mess up type. Hopefully, this chapter has shown the damage to legibility each of those errors can inflict.

21st Century Book Cover Design

CHAPTER 9:
Deadly Sin of Cover Design #5 Complexity

9.1 Montages

In the past, a common illustrative technique used on book covers was the montage. They required a skilled practitioner but offered multiple sub-images that might intrigue a reader. They continue to be used in a wide variety of applications such as movie posters and magazine covers and interior illustrations.

But for modern book covers montages are no longer as useful as they once were. The issue is size. At a size of 160 pixels high for the typical first viewing, covers with montages have too many parts that just are too tiny to be discernible. As such, they are very rarely used now, and with good reason; they just don't work that small.

9.2 Simplicity

A cover can not spell out all of what a book is about, nor should it try to, for it will fail. Even the plot of the simplest novel could never be spelled out in any single image. Better instead to reach for what can be achieved. A wise designer will try to communicate something of the mood, genre or characters of the book in as simple a way as possible.

We have said before that "Less Is More" and "Simplicity is the Soul of Good Design." Unfortunately, many agree outwardly with this idea but have failed to be converted to its reality.

Each of these book covers is more powerful for its simplicity. This is so important when the first cover anyone is likely to see is only 160 pixels high. Of all these, the weakest is the second from the top left because it lacks even one element with excellent contrast.

Of course, it takes great skill to render a book to its essence. When selling books in the 21st century, simplicity is not just nice to do. It can be the secret to success.

CHAPTER 10:

Deadly Sin of Cover Design #6 Poor use of Space

10.1 Element Hierarchy

One of the elements of good design is hierarchy. This means that in any truly effective design, one element will be the focal point, a different element will come in second, and another will be third. If two elements try to both be dominant, the design will be weaker for it. Size is a common determinant of dominance but it is not the only factor. A smaller item at a greater contrast can often end up as the dominant element. On book covers there are usually only three or four elements: Title, Author, Image, and sometimes a Subtitle, book series number or a teaser line about the plot. From so few elements, one should be the dominant, one the secondary and so forth.

10.2 Blocking

The act of breaking up a design by enclosing elements in sub shapes within the picture plane is inherently an inefficient use of space. Most often type within such a sub-shape has a margin between it and the shape edges and the shapes need a certain buffer of space between themselves and other elements. In such cases space is wasted on double margins, where it could be better used with single margins or buffers and larger elements. Using unnecessary shapes also makes the overall image more complex with little benefit. If values need to be adjusted, a less intrusive and wasteful alternative is to feather images and use soft overlays to lighten or darken backgrounds under type.

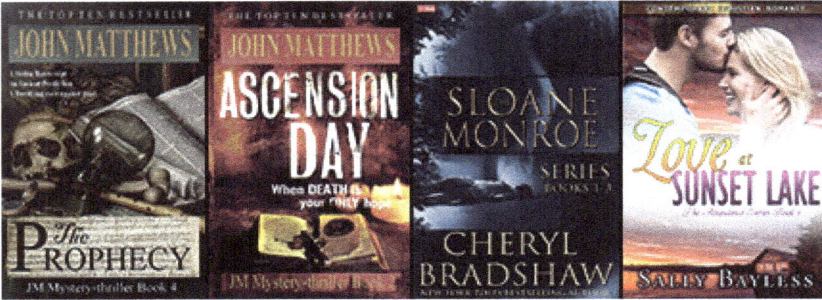

1. The title block is interruptive to the carefully arranged subject and requires the title type to be smaller than it could be without the block. **2.** The contrast for the author's name here (and in 1 also) is lessened by a mid value block. The author's names in both cases could have been both bigger and easier to read without the blocks behind them. **3.** The blocks interfere with the background image with no real benefit to the type. **4.** Preferable to using blocks would be the soft value shifts used here. The line of type at the top would have been better served with same technique, or even better, that type could have been flush right and nested in the top right section without going over the man's head at all.

10.3 Wasting Space

Given how important it is to have a legible title and author's name, the wasting of space is such a short-sighted decision. While a canvas 6" x 9" may seem generous enough that a little wasted space will not be noticed, the reality of modern book marketing really means your canvas is only about one inch tall or even shorter. Every effort should

1. Given the nature of the photo, there was no need for the blue box at the bottom; the black of the trees could have been extended. But even without that, both title and author's name could have been increased in size. **2.** Given how dark and large the space at the top of the illustration is, there was no need for the title to be as small as it is. The illustration could also have been moved up to allow space for a bigger author's name. **3.** This photo could have been enlarged with the empty part at left leaving the picture plane. The title could also have been enlarged. **4.** Title type could have been twice as big and author's name is ridiculously small while there is empty space proclaiming what a boring cover this is.

be made to increase the type size as far as space will allow. Wasted space means less readable type, which, in turn results in fewer interested shoppers.

10.4 Crowding
The height of design clumsiness is demonstrated when visual elements are unnecessarily crowded. With Photoshop at one's disposal and the almost infinite choice of type styles, there is no reason to ever have to cover over important visual elements, much less a natural focal point on a cover.

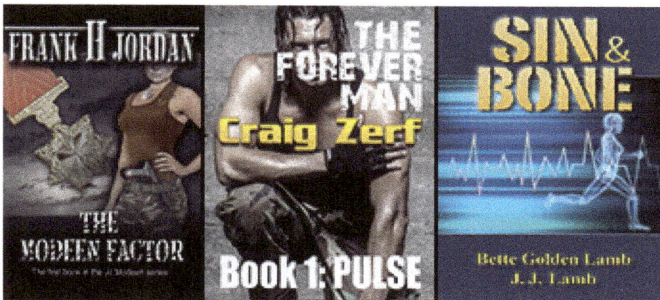

1. There was more than enough space at the bottom for the picture to have been lowered to let us see all of the woman's face. It is a natural focal point and partly covering it does not create suspense, it's just irksome. **2.** Covering the man's face makes no sense at all here. Neither does having the "Book 1: PULSE" larger than either the title or the author's name. **3.** There was room at the bottom to move down the image so that the running figure would not crowd the title type.

CHAPTER 11:

Deadly Sin of Cover Design #7 Poor Imagery

11. Image Contrast

We have referred to contrast in type at length and shown several different ways that this can be compromised, thus robbing the text of legibility. We have also seen that what looks like modest legibility at a larger size can become altogether unreadable at a reduced size.

The same principles apply to images. Internal contrast is necessary in order to "read" an image. As with type, any deficiencies in image contrast magnify their negative effects when reduced in size. A focal point especially needs to have good contrast.

Proper art direction of photographers and illustrators can prevent much of this from happening.

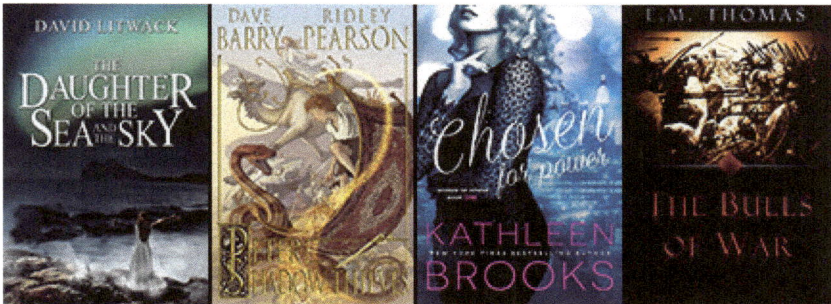

1. This image's focal point is a woman standing near a rocky shore with her arms outstretched; but her dress is light against light water and her upper body is in shadow against a dark set of rocks. Those should be switched: her dress should be dark and her arms light. **2.** This very well executed illustration has the hero's light face (the natural focal point) against the light body of a camel. If the camel's body were dark it would make all the difference, giving contrast for the hero's face. **3.** The photo has good contrast but the background has unnecessary white flare dots that can be confusing at first viewing. Also the middle right background is too busy for the title and the bottom should be darkened to give more contrast to the author's name. **4.** Instead of the all-to-common low contrast, this image is in such high contrast that it is hard to figure out what it is. A tighter cropped image enlarged with fewer elements and normal contrast would be better.

11.2 Mismatched Imagery

Photoshop is an amazing tool. With it, and the right know-how, one can fix some aspects of a defective image or combine things that originally were separate. But it can not do everything.

One basic principle of professional imagery is to not mix styles or overt techniques. It draws attention to itself and takes all harmony away from the end product. Even when just mixing photos, if you are attempting to create a scene from multiple sources, be sure the lighting is consistent and all comes from the same direction.

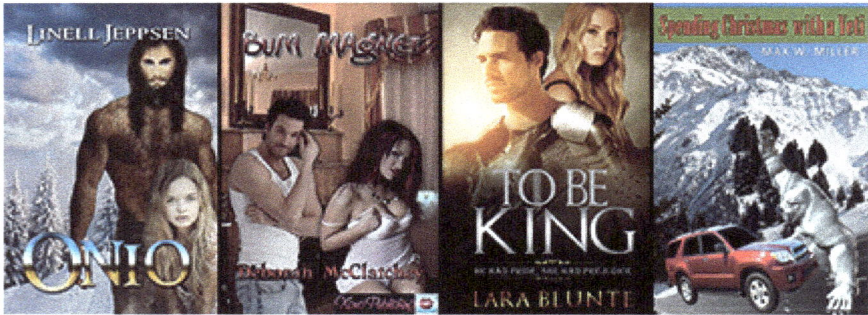

1. The light in the background landscape comes from the right but the woman's face is in diffused light. The hairy man is obviously illustrated or a heavily edited photo (not too well done). The end result does not hold together well. **2.** The lighting on the man and woman here are very different and the background gives poor contrast for them and the title type. **3.** We might suppose the man to be a medieval knight, but if he is, the small shoulder strap on the woman looks anachronistic. **4.** This hodgepodge assemblage of images fails to look like a real scene and is laughably hokey. And what is the purpose of the green stripe under the red title type? It offers no better contrast to the red type than the blue sky would have; white type would have been better.

11.3 Amateur Imagery

As we said at the beginning, people do judge a book by its cover. We also said that "Just because you eat every day doesn't meant you know how to cook." We all can tell what amateur imagery is. How strange that some self publishers can not. But it broadcasts to all that this book is not likely to be of a standard that they might hope. Of course, writing is a separate skill from art—or art direction, for that matter. But this one truth should be remembered: better to have no imagery than bad imagery. Plenty of successful books have no imagery on their covers. Better to reach for less and accomplish it than reach for more and fail.

If you wonder whether someone else will notice the deficiencies of an image that you are considering for a book cover, be assured that enough people will, indeed, notice—if not consciously, then subliminally—and reject your book because of it.

I have signed up for a daily email newsletter posting of Amazon Kindle books that are offered at a reduced price or even for free sometimes. But just because a book is free does not mean I will bother to download it, even if it is in my favorite genre, not if the cover is amateurish. It's not worth my time because I do judge a book by its cover. And so do most people.

I repeat: the cover is the single most important page in any book.

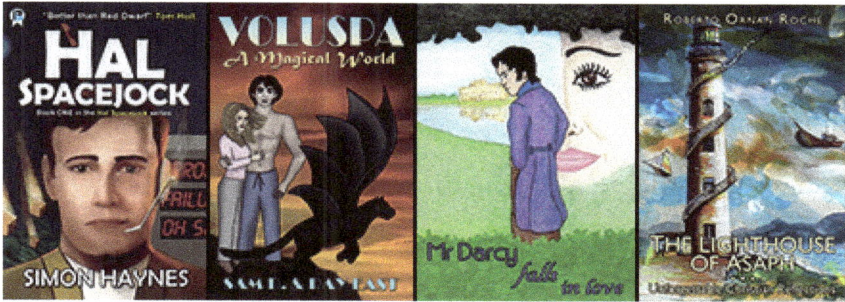

Look at the top 100 books on Amazon in your particular genre. How many use illustration at all? How many use such techniques as outlined forms, pencil and watercolor? Then why would you? Do not be so blindly foolish as to suppose that you will set a trend. Instead learn from your genre. Then meet its expectations. And above all, only use professional grade imagery.

CHAPTER 12:
Word to Publishers, Traditional and Indie

In the world marketplace, the most important single page on any book is its cover. And the nature of successful covers in 21st century marketing has changed. This has been the whole premise of this book.

12.1 Ebook Pricing

There are still plenty of folks who prefer to have a book made of paper in their hands rather than reading on an ebook reader and they are still the majority of readers. But that majority is declining.

Naturally, the lack of up-front costs for digital books has been a big boon to the self publishing world. The Amazon royalty split for ebooks is also much more favorable. For the average ebook with a sale price between 99¢ and $2.98, the royalty payment to authors is as much as 35%. For ebooks over $2.99 and under $9.99 the royalty paid to authors is 70%.

Beyond that, there are significant expenses for traditionally published paper books sold through brick and mortar bookstores compared to selling ebooks online. The biggest saving in producing ebooks are:

• No printing costs for ebooks
• No warehouse storage costs for ebooks
• No shipping costs to the brick and mortar bookstores
• No discounting the wholesale price to the store by 55%
• No return of books*

*Most people outside of the book industry do not know that a bookstore ordering books from a major publisher has a whole year to return those books for a full refund. Not only that, the bookstore does not actually return those books so the publisher can resell them. Bookstores only have to rip off the covers on paperback books and send those back. The publishers do not get back any books; those are a complete loss for the publisher. This is undoubtedly the highest cost for books that aren't assured of selling out at the store.

One has to wonder: why do the major publishers not charge significantly less for ebooks than print books? With all of those above costs not incurred, ebooks have to be so much more profitable for them compared to print books. Still, most of the big five publishing conglomerates charge close to the print price for their ebooks. Inexplicably, a few publishers charge more for their ebooks than their print books.

When queried, these companies make vague reference to "other costs" incurred before printing such as editing and promotion. These so-called "other" costs do not hold up to scrutiny. Editing is not a major expense and very few books in a publisher's list ever get much in the way of advertising.

As a result, consumers recognize those publishers are ripping them off and are voting with their purses and taking a chance on the $2.99 self published ebook instead of paying $8 to $15 for a traditionally published ebook.

Ebook market share for the Big Five publishers has plummeted since they took back setting their own (exorbitant) prices. Between February 2014 and May 2015, only fifteen months, the Big Five publishers and Indie Publishers traded places for market share of unit

Ebook Unit Sales Market Share

Big Five Publishers compared to Indie Publishers

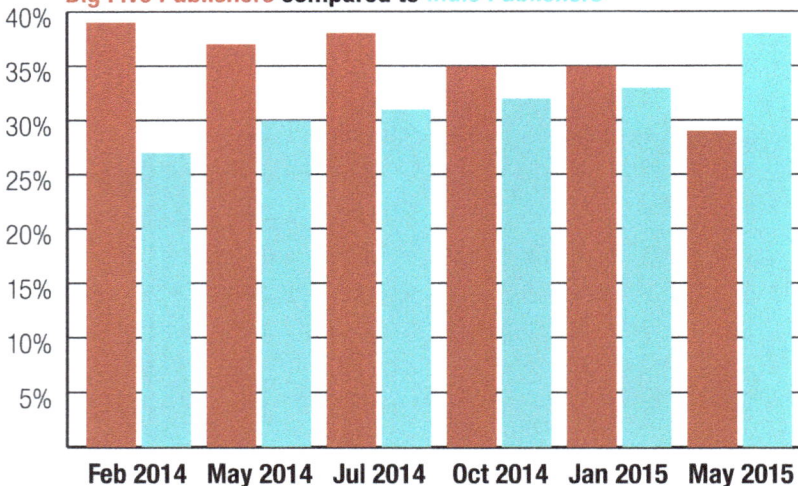

sales of ebooks. The biggest factor in this is thought to be their respective prices.

While the Big Five publishing houses insist on charging higher prices for their ebooks, sometimes as much or more than for their printed books, the marketplace has welcomed indie publishers as never before.

In fact, as of this writing, indie authors receive fully half of the author royalties in the US for the entire book industry—up from 35% only two years ago. Part of this is because indie authors often get as much as 40% of the sale price of print books, and up to 70% for ebooks, whereas traditionally published authors typically only get 10% or less on average. However, considering that the average indie ebook sells for quite a bit less than those of the Big Five publishing empires, it is an even more impressive statistic.

12.2 Amazon Can't Be Ignored

Folks either love Amazon or hate it. Whereas Apple has the avowed goal to be the most innovative company on the planet (and seem to be delivering on that promise), Amazon wants to be the most customer-centric company on the planet. Speaking for myself, as a customer, I am very pleased with Amazon.

19.5% of all books sold in the US are Kindle titles

Total US Ebook Sales

Apple, Barnes & Noble, Google, Kobo

amazon

65%

Source: Forbes 2014

And no one can deny the way they have led the ebook revolution. Now about one fifth of all book unit sales in the US are Kindle sales. iTunes, Barnes and Noble, Kobo and Google sharing the remaining one third of ebook sales.

12.3 The Age of Self-Publishing

Ebooks aren't the only venue for self published authors. PoD or Print on Demand books have also increased in quality and decreased in price to such a degree that it is a competitive alternative to printing books in lots of thousands to provide physical books to the market. Amazon's CreateSpace was and continues to be a leader in this arena. They have now been joined by IngramSpark, LightningSource, BookBaby and others that make this a viable option. Books are not printed until an order is placed. This avoids any storage costs, not to mention investing in print runs of multiple thousands of books. The profit per book is much less but the up-front investment (and risk) is also very little. When book sales reach a steady level, the publisher can switch over to more traditional and profitable print runs (which most of these same companies can also offer).

As a result of all this, indie publishing (self published books) is taking off. Some authors also create their own publishing companies even though they still only publish their own work. This sector of self published authors are known by

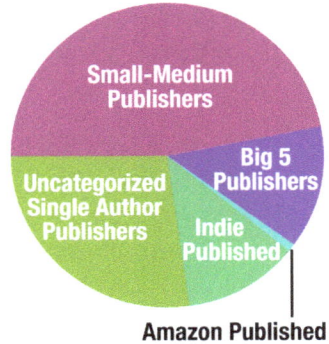

US Ebook Market Shares
By Publisher Type

(Source: AuthorEarnings.com - Jan 2016)

a separate but less than brief title "Uncategorized Single Author Publishers." Together these two segments account for just over one third of the whole book market in terms of sales units. The Big Five publishing conglomerates no longer dominate the world of book publishing, either in print or ebooks.

12.4 Not a Game for Amateurs

Getting published traditionally used to be the only practical method for becoming a successful author. Even way back then (ten years ago?) only one in fifty authors could quit the proverbial day job and rely on book royalties for a decent living. Even fewer became the rich celebs that we see on our favorite talk shows. So now, yes, the playing field has been leveled, but book publishing is still not a place where any old book will succeed. The challenge before was (and still is in traditional publishing) getting both an agent and an editor to believe in your work to get you published.

Now you can write just about any junk and self publish it (and many thousands do). The challenge today is no longer to get published, but rather to get noticed in the sea of books.

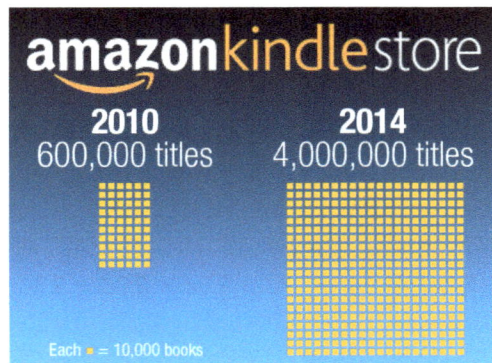

amazonkindle store

2010
600,000 titles

2014
4,000,000 titles

Each ■ = 10,000 books

The veritable tidal wave of books is daunting. In 2010 there were 600,000 titles in the Kindle Store. Only four years later, there were 400,000 titles. Now, only two years later that number has almost doubled again!

Combining ebooks and printed books, traditionally published and indie, it is estimated that Amazon alone carries over 1.8 million different titles.

There are many tens of thousands of books available that no agent said were good enough to be published; no professional editor said they were good enough to be published. How do people find the worthwhile stuff amidst all that schlock?

Potential readers can use recommendations from friends, like-minded readers, reviews, and blogs to direct their hunting. Best seller lists alone could keep most of us in good reading material perpetually. But how do books get on that best seller list to begin with?

We've answered this before: word-of-mouth.

Then how do we get those first readers to buy and read our book so they will start the word-of-mouth chain reaction?

First is really great, unparalleled content.

Second is a great cover.

A poor book with a great cover may get a few readers but it will not succeed in the long run. If the book is mediocre or poor it will not find much of a readership. On the other hand, a first rate book with a second rate cover may also be doomed, if not to failure, at least to a great deal less than it could have done with a good cover.

12.5 Moving Forward

The principles in this book are not magic nor are they only for a certain gifted few. They may be learned by anyone who is willing to work at it. Even so, after reading this book and considering things you may not have thought about before, you may realize that there will be, as in any art form, a certain learning curve.

You may decide to engage a graphic designer. Do not suppose that every graphic designer understands the principles in this book. Many of our negative examples in this book came from the big publishing houses who employ real graphic designers. It should be obvious, therefore, that just being a graphic designer does not mean that person understands these principles.

If you are going to hire someone to do your book cover(s), why not loan them your copy of this book? It can only help your end product.

People do indeed judge books by their covers. And following these principles, there is no need to ever have a cover that fails, even at one inch high.

Appendix
Covers of A. Michael Shumate

I have been writing and publishing books for some years and not
wholly avoiding some of the same pitfalls mentioned in this book.
Still, I aspire, as I hope you do now as well, to better covers going
forward. The principles are logical and hold up to scrutiny as well as
practical use. Let us all be wiser in the future.

Other Books by

A. Michael Shumate

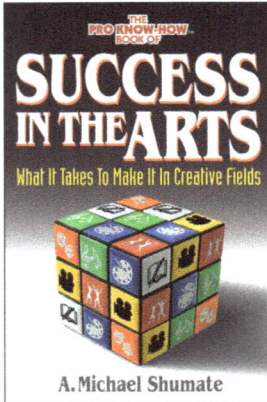

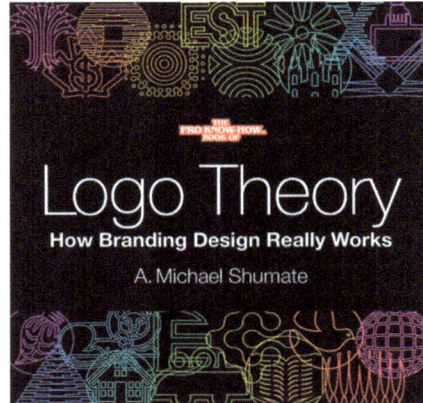

For: Writers, Musicians, Filmmakers, Visual Artists, Dancers, Actors

Learn This Essential Knowledge:

- What factors contribute most to success in the arts?
- Do you have enough talent?
- What do you need besides talent?
- Learn the four myths about creativity.
- What real creativity is; how to grow it.
- How to get through tough times.
- How do you deal with criticism.
- How to "get the breaks" in your field.
- What basic principles don't change?
- How to hang on to the important things in life and keep from "selling your soul."
- What if you don't make it?
- Save years of trial and error
- Avoid common pitfalls of creative careers.
- A mentor in a book

Available in print and for Kindle from Amazon.com

"At last somebody actually understands what identity design is all about and how it is accomplished."
– *Ivan Chermayeff*
Chermayeff & Geismar & Haviv, NYC

- There principles of corporate identity design that don't change, principles that transcend fad and fashion.
- Learn why some corporate identities have been used for decades, some for more than half a century, and still look contemporary, while others look dated and tired in only a few years.
- There only four different corporate identity concepts. Learn how that can help generate more and better concepts.
- Avoid the Seven Deadly Sins of Logo Design.
- Save years of fruitless trial and error. See with clear, real world examples, with your own eyes concepts and principles not found in any other book on branding design.

Available at bookstores and online booksellers everywhere

www.ingramcontent.com/pod-product-compliance
Lightning Source LLC
Chambersburg PA
CBHW041301040426
42334CB00028BA/3119